A BEGINNER'S METHOD FOR CREATING POWERF[UL]

C·R·A·W·L

BEFO[RE YOU] WALK

MW00594223

BY TOM WARRINGTON

I'd like to thank two great musicians, Steve Houghton and Bill Cunliffe; Tallie Sherwood for his great engineering; and special thanks to Link Harnsberger, Dave Black, Ron Manus, Tom Gerou, Kim Kasabian, Greg Plumblee, the team at Alfred Publishing, Rudy at Foxfire Studios and Meiko Powers for her support.

On acoustic bass, Tom plays Thomastik-Infeld Strings.

Interior photographs: Larry Lydle

2

TABLE OF CONTENTS

USING THIS CD

This CD has been recorded with the bass track entirely on the left channel so that by dialing the balance control on your stereo all the way to the right, the bass track can be completely eliminated. By doing this, you can play along with just the piano and drums, like a real band situation. If you have doubts about what to play, dial the balance control back to the center and listen to the given track. Then dial it out and insert your own playing.

Each track on the CD begins with eight "free" beats ahead of the actual music: four clicks, followed by a spoken count-off, "one-two-three-four." This is to give the tempo and to show exactly where the beats are so you can start playing exactly together with the CD at the beginning of each example.

To get the most benefit from this CD, use a cassette recorder to record yourself playing with the CD while the bass track is dialed out. Then you can play back the recording you've just made and really hear how you sound playing with the band! This is a lot of fun and a very useful learning tool, so please experiment with it.

3

FOREWORD

The goal of this book is to show students and teachers alike an easy pathway to creating powerful walking bass lines from chord charts, and to do it in a fun way that avoids the foreboding topics of music theory and sight-reading. After finishing this book, a student should be able to read a chart with chord changes and play a solid, good quality bass line. In addition, teachers who have read the book will better understand how to start a beginning bass student. The book includes step-by-step instructions and a fundamental play-along CD, so I will literally be right there to help you along as you explore this easy method for playing great bass lines.

ABOUT THE AUTHOR

After receiving his master's degree in composition from the University of Illinois, Tom moved to New York City in the mid 1970s. There he quickly got the call to join the Buddy Rich Band, a stint that lasted over two years. After that period, he toured Europe extensively as a performer and clinician, and worked with many other great NY artists including Stan Getz, Dave Liebman, and Hank Jones.

Tom came to Los Angeles in 1981, and has performed and recorded with a long list of great artists, including Freddie Hubbard, Terry Trotter, Peter Erskine, Denny Zeitlin, Bob Florence, Lenny Niehaus, Mose Allison, Arturo Sandoval, and many others. His playing can be heard on over 100 recordings spanning a wide range of styles. Tom has also played on many movie and television scores, and is a featured artist on the soundtrack of Jodie Foster's film *Little Man Tate*. He has also performed at the renowned Playboy Jazz Festival with Randy Brecker's quintet at the Hollywood Bowl, and with Billy Childs at the Montreal and North Sea Jazz Festivals. Recently, he has also recorded live CDs with trombone legend Carl Fontana and with jazz trumpet great Conte Candoli.

Tom continues to play and record with top jazz players, and his articulate communication methods have made him a top choice as clinician at festivals and conventions. Writing also plays an increasing role in his activities. In addition to jingle orchestrations and vocal jazz charts, Tom has co-authored *Essential Styles*, books one and two as well as an instructional video series, *The Contemporary Rhythm Section*, and the book/CD play-along series, *MasterTracks*.

As a beginning bass player, there are a few essential things to learn right away. This information falls into two categories: basic music stuff, and playing this instrument called the bass. Let's start with some basic music.

BASIC MUSIC STUFF

Music is written on a five-line staff, and we put notes on this staff to show two things: the pitch we want to hear, and the length of time it should last. For example, in bass clef, the lines of the staff indicate the notes G, B, D, F and A from bottom to top, and the spaces between the lines indicate the notes A, C, E and G. To remember this, I was taught "Good Boys Do Fine Always," and "All Cows Eat Grass."

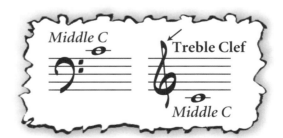

"Bass clef" was mentioned earlier. A clef is a sign at the beginning of the staff that shows what range the pitches are in so that they fall mostly within the staff. There are several different clefs, and the one you use depends on whether you are playing high notes, low notes, or in-between notes. For example, in bass clef the note "middle-C" (the C in the middle of the piano keyboard) is the line just above the staff, so the notes that fall within the staff will all sound lower than middle C. This is the clef we use, because we play low notes. A flute player would read treble clef, where middle-C is the line just below the staff, and all the notes that fall in the staff sound above middle-C. See the example below.

That takes care of pitch, but what about the length of the notes? Well, there are lots of different kinds of notes, but if you understand a bit about fractions, it's easy. There are whole notes, half notes, quarter notes, eighth notes, and sixteenth notes. (There are others, but these are the most common.) A whole note equals two half notes or four quarter notes, just like a dollar equals two half-dollars or four quarters.

whole note (semibreve)

half note (minim)

quarter note (crotchet)

eighth note (quaver)

sixteenth note (semiquaver)

whole rest (semibreve rest)

half rest (minim rest)

quarter rest (crotchet rest)

eighth rest (quaver rest)

sixteenth rest (semiquaver rest)

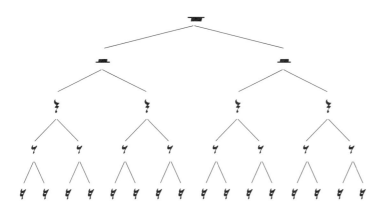

Go back to the beginning and play again.

In order to make it easy to keep your place, music is divided into measures, which are small chunks of time. Each measure contains some beats, and the time signature (those numbers at the beginning of the music) tells us how it all works. For example, with a $\frac{4}{4}$ time signature, the top 4 tells us that there are four beats in each measure, and the bottom 4 tells us that a quarter note gets one beat. So, it would take four quarter notes to make one complete measure of music in $\frac{4}{4}$ time. Most walking bass lines will consist mainly of quarter notes in $\frac{4}{4}$ time.

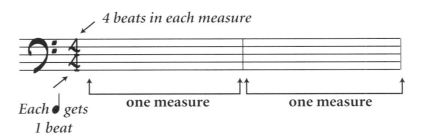

Much of the music in this book will have only chord symbols and some slash marks, like this:

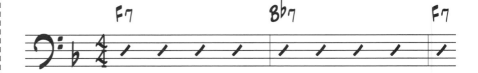

The slash marks show the beats, and the chord symbol tells us which chord should be played. Most of the time, the chord will change on the downbeat, which is the first beat of the measure. As a bass player, you will have to be able to read both notes and chord symbols. The notes tell you exactly what to play and when, but chord symbol notation leaves note choices up to you. In other words, if you see:

you know that you have to play some notes for four beats that fit with a B♭ chord, but exactly which notes to play is your choice. Helping you make those choices and play a good-sounding walking bass line is what this book is all about.

Okay, that covers some very basic musical info, so let's talk about the bass itself. Some of you will be playing acoustic bass, and others will be playing electric bass, so I will cover some basic technique on both instruments.

First, the position of the hands on both instruments is very important. Take a look at the pictures on the next two pages, and compare them to your own hand position:

BASIC TECHNIQUE

Standing with electric bass

Sitting with electric bass

Standing with acoustic bass

Sitting with acoustic bass

Left hand on electric bass

Right hand on electric bass

Left hand on acoustic bass

Both hands should feel natural and relaxed, and the wrists should not be bent too much. The left hand thumb should support the fingers, so that the pressure to push the string down is between the thumb and the finger. Be careful not to let the left hand collapse so that the palm or heel of the hand is supporting the finger pressure. This is very important! The thumb should never be "peaking" around the front of the neck, but should always be behind it, supporting the fingers. This will help you to hold down each note until you play the next one, so that your bass line sounds smooth and connected, not like a bunch of short, choppy notes.

On acoustic bass, the right hand plucks the strings over the bottom end of the fingerboard. To imitate this sound on electric bass, it makes sense to pluck the string over the end of the fingerboard, rather than back by the bridge. Experiment with this a bit. Pluck some notes by the bridge, over the fingerboard, and at all points in between, and notice the difference in sound.

It's important to get familiar with your instrument, so before you try to do anything, just play some notes and mess around with the bass. Play some high notes, some low ones, play loud and soft, try to pick out a little melody, and just get acquainted with how the bass feels and what it sounds like. Maybe you can even put on a CD and try to play along! Have some fun, and then you'll be ready to go on with *Crawl Before You Walk*.

Right hand on acoustic bass

The first thing you need to do when you pull the bass out of the case is to tune it up so that it matches the pitch on the CD. The open strings, from the lowest pitched, fattest one, are E, A, D and G. Check the pitches on your bass and be sure that they match the pitches on the CD.

 Track 1

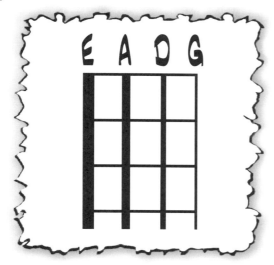

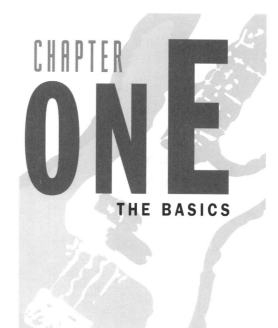

Now we're ready to get started. The first two things that are important to learn are where the notes are on the bass, and what their names are. For now, we will learn just a few notes on each string. The following diagram shows each string with the open string note-name at the top, and the note names for each of the first three frets (or positions, if you're playing fretless or acoustic bass). Look at this diagram closely; play these notes and listen to them until you really feel comfortable and confident that you know where these notes are.

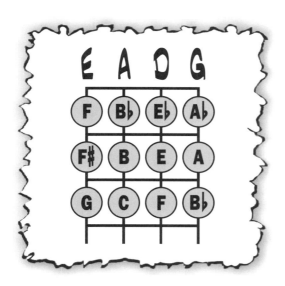

The chord progression we will be using is a basic 12-bar blues progression. It's a good place to start because it is a very common form that's short and simple. A blues chord chart might look like this:

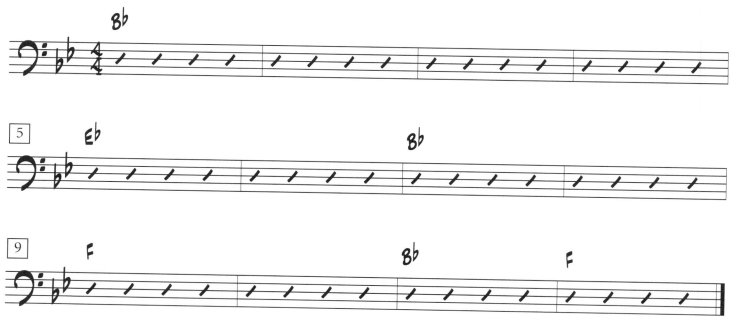

Look at the chart and you will see chord symbols and a bunch of little slashes. Each slash represents one beat, so if we're counting "1—2—3—4—" you would have one slash on each count. We're going to practice playing a note on "one" which is the first beat, or "downbeat." Let's start with B♭. Cue up the CD to Track 2. Listen to the count off, keep track of the counts in your head, and play a B♭ on every "one." If you were to write it out, it would look like Track 2 below, but for now, just listen to the CD and try to make your note happen exactly on the downbeat. Do it along with the existing bass track, then dial out my bass track and try it on your own with just the piano and drums. This is exactly how it will feel when you are the bass player in a band!

TRACK 2

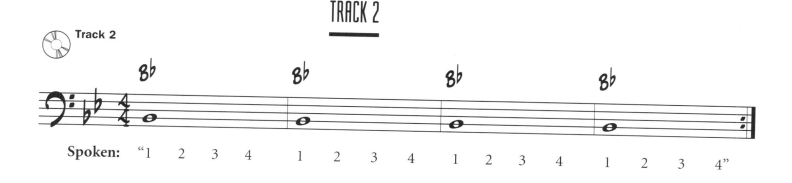

When you feel comfortable with this, it's time to move into working with the blues progression. What we're going to do, very slowly at first, is to play a *chord root* on every downbeat. A chord root is nothing more than the note the chord is named for. So, a Bb chord has Bb as the root, an Eb chord has Eb as the root, and so forth. Take a look at the blues chart, and find out how many different chord roots there are. In this simple progression there are three different chords, and as a result, three different chord roots: Bb, Eb and F. Take your bass and find all of these notes. Refer back to the diagram that shows where the notes are on the bass if you need to.

Now look at the chart below. We're going to do exactly what we did in Track 2—play a note on each downbeat—only now we're going to play a different note sometimes; we're going to play the root of each chord whenever the chord changes. You can tell when the chord changes by following along on the chart along with the music on the CD. Tracks 3 and 4 are both the same 12-bar blues progression played over and over, but work with Track 3 for a while at first because it's slow, and you can more easily get the hang of playing along. Play right along with me at first, then, when you feel comfortable, dial out the bass track on the CD and try it on your own. When Track 3 feels slow, move on to Track 4, which is a little faster.

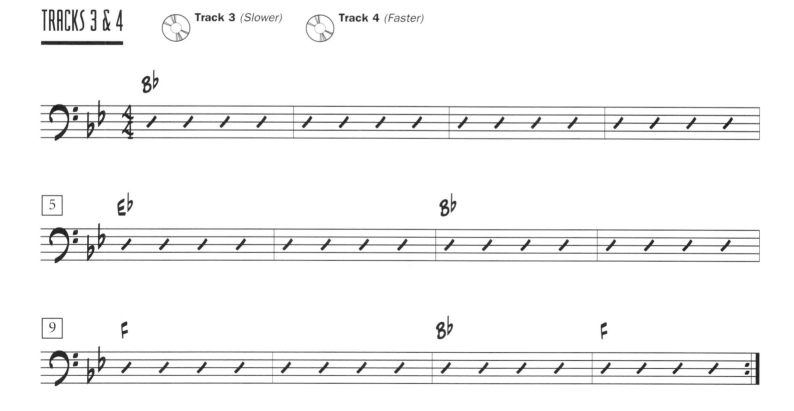

TRACKS 3 & 4   **Track 3** *(Slower)*   **Track 4** *(Faster)*

Good job....you're well on your way!

CHAPTER
TWO
THE NEXT STEP

Now that you have a good feel for this progression, let's go on to the next two examples. The progression is exactly the same, only now, instead of playing notes just on beat one, we're going to play notes on beats one *and three*. This feel is called "2-beat" because we're playing two beats in each measure. If it were written out with notes, it would look like this:

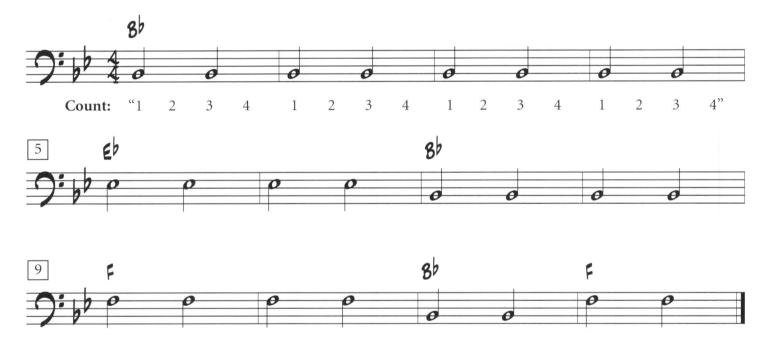

Now listen to Track 5 on the CD, and try to play along with it. We aren't adding any different notes, we're just playing an extra chord root on beat three in each measure.

Also, just a word about technique: try to make each note sound warm and full, and hold each note out until you play the next one, so there isn't a big space between the notes. When you feel comfortable with Track 5, move on to Track 6, which is a little bit faster. Again, play right along with me at first, then, when you feel comfortable, dial out the bass track on the CD and try it on your own.

TRACKS 5 & 6

 **Track 5** *(Slower)*    **Track 6** *(Faster)*

Playing with steady time is *very important*, so listen as you play along with the bass track on the CD, and try to play your notes at exactly the same time as the notes on the track. Then, when you tune out the bass track, listen to the ride cymbal beat, and try to play your notes so that they line up with the cymbal notes on beats one and three. This is not as easy as it sounds, especially when you have to do it for a longer time. So, listen carefully and really try to feel the pulse in the cymbal beat and play right with it. Remember, playing the right notes is of no value if they aren't played at the *right time*.

This would be a great time to begin recording yourself. Play the CD and dial out the bass channel, then record yourself playing along with the piano and drum tracks on the CD. Listen back and see how you sound; listen to how your notes are lining up with the cymbal beat. Playing a part that fits with a previously recorded track is something we are often called on to do in the studio, so this is really great practice!

CHAPTER THREE

$\frac{4}{4}$ TIME

Now it's time to get to the real heart of the matter; playing four quarter notes in each measure–a note on each beat. Here again, the idea of lining up the notes with the drummer's cymbal beat is *very* important (see the diagram below). Also, the notes should flow *evenly* from one to the next, with each note having the same length, so that the line forms a smooth rhythmic pulse, like a heart beat.

Ride cymbal:

Bass notes:

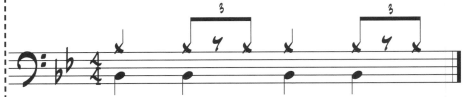

We will use the same basic blues progression as in the 2-beat example, only now we will play *four* notes in each measure, one note on each beat. This will be tricky, so the first example is nice and slow to let you get the feel of it. Stay lined up with the cymbal beat, and concentrate on keeping your place in the form so you know which chord is coming next. This means you have to know two things at all times: first, which beat you are playing (1, 2, 3, or 4), and second, which measure of the form you are playing. It seems like a lot to keep in mind, but it will begin to sound and feel more natural to you as you keep playing this progression.

Just listen to Track 7 a couple times to see how it works, then play along with me. Listen to the sound and length of my notes, and try to make your notes sound the same way. When you've got the feel of it, turn off my bass channel and go it alone with the drums and piano.

 **Track 7** *(Slower)*  **Track 8** *(Faster)*

Track 8 is more of the same thing, only faster. You should go ahead with Track 8 only after you have played Track 7 a bunch of times without mistakes and are feeling really comfortable. Do the same routine: play with me at first and try to imitate the sound, then tune me out and play with piano and drums. This might be a good time to record yourself playing along with the drum and piano tracks, then listen back to what you've done and see how it sounds to you. Compare it to the original with my bass track. Make a note of anything you played that you don't like so that you can work on improving it. Don't go on to the next chapter until you have really mastered everything in this chapter.

Congratulations! You have just played your first walking bass line!

CHAPTER FOUR

EASY PASSING TONES

Congratulations again on playing a walking bass line! Now that you have the ability to play chord roots on all four beats, let's add to what you've learned and explore some easy ways to make your bass lines more interesting.

What is a passing tone? It is nothing more than a note that is played as we "pass" from one chord to another; sort of an in-between note. The first type of passing tone we will use is called a *leading tone. The leading tone is found ½ step (one fret) below the chord root that it leads to.* For example, in the Bb blues, we start on the chord Bb. As we move to the next chord, Eb, the tone that "leads" us there is D, which is ½ step below Eb. The next chord in the progression is F, and we can lead to F from ½ step below it, the note E. Finally, we return to Bb from the note A, which is ½ step below Bb. Let's put these notes into our chord chart so we can see exactly where they go.

As you can see in the chart below, all of the chords are circled, and the leading tones that take us to the chord roots from the ½ step below are shown in brackets. Note that in measures 2 and 3,

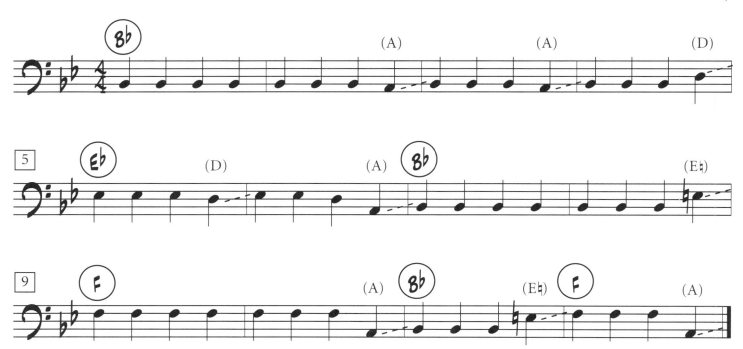

I used a couple extra leading tones, going from A to B♭. This is just for a little extra variety, since we have four whole measures of B♭, but you don't have to play those notes if you don't want to. The most important leading tones are the ones that take us to a new chord. So, you will play all chord roots as before, only now you will play a leading tone on the fourth beat as we move to a new chord.

TRACKS 9 & 10

Before you begin to play with these next tracks, take a minute to locate the new notes on your bass. We've already been playing B♭, E♭ and F, so the new notes are each ¹/₂ step (one fret) below these notes that are familiar. Compare your bass neck to the diagram and find the leading tones D, E and A. Notice that all of these leading notes *could* be played on open strings. Just make sure that you play the leading tone on beat "4" and go up a ¹/₂ step to the next chord root on beat "1" of the next measure.

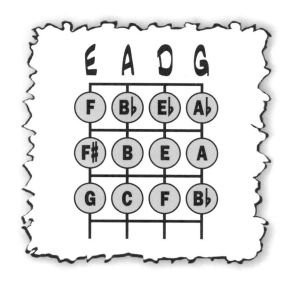

Listen to Track 9 a couple of times to hear how the leading tones work, then play along with me. When you feel comfortable, turn off the bass channel and play by yourself with the piano and drum track. **Advanced tip:** Notice that the passing tone/chord root combination A to B♭ is found in *two* places on the fingerboard— on the G string (2nd & 3rd fret) and on the A string (open and 1st fret)...try to use both locations. As before, the first example (Track 9) is nice and slow, and the second one (Track 10) is a bit faster. Practice these many times!

Track 9 *(Slower)*   **Track 10** *(Faster)*

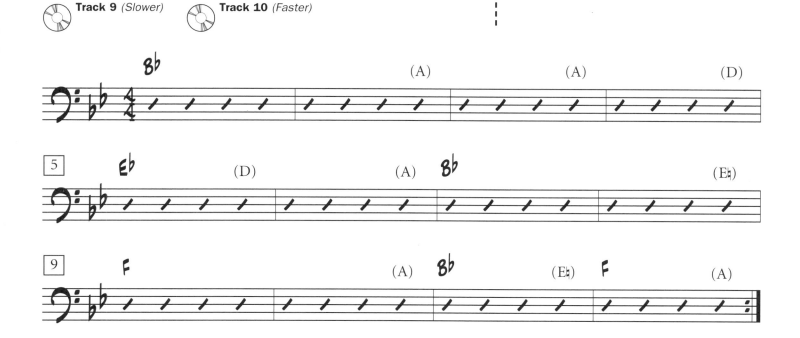

TRACKS 11 & 12

Another kind of passing tone approaches the next chord root from *¹/₂ step above it*. Again, take a look at the neck diagram or your own bass neck and locate the notes ¹/₂ step above our familiar notes B♭, E♭ and F. They are B, E and F♯ (G♭). Now, we're going to do exactly what we did on the last two examples, except that we will move to each new chord root from *¹/₂ step above it, instead of ¹/₂ step below it*.

Again, listen to Track 11 to hear how the approach tones sound, then play along with me. When you feel comfortable, turn off the bass channel and play along with just the piano and drums. **Advanced tip:** Notice that the approach tone/chord root combinations B to B♭ and F♯ to F are found in *two* places on the fingerboard; find where they are, and try to use both locations.

Track 11 *(Slower)*   **Track 12** *(Faster)*

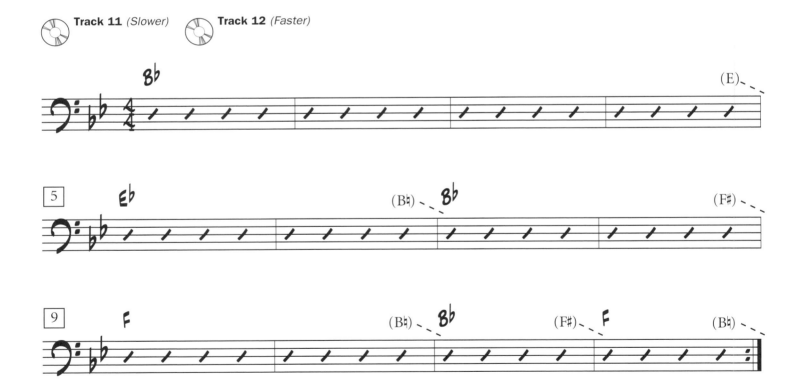

TRACKS 13 & 14 ● COMBINING PASSING TONES

Now that you can move freely from chord to chord from either $\frac{1}{2}$ step above or $\frac{1}{2}$ step below, it's time to combine these two concepts. This time, as you go through the chord changes, it will be your decision whether to approach the next chord from $\frac{1}{2}$ step above or $\frac{1}{2}$ step below! So listen to what I do on the next two tracks, then dial me out and play with the piano and drum tracks. I want you to be free to decide which passing tones to use on your own, rather than copying what I played. Just use my playing as a guide, then go on your own! Use the chart below if you want to; the places to use passing tones are marked "PT." Notice also that there is one extra chord in this version of the blues, an E♭ in measure 10, which makes this progression more like those found in rock and R&B music.

Track 13 *(Slower)* **Track 14** *(Faster)*

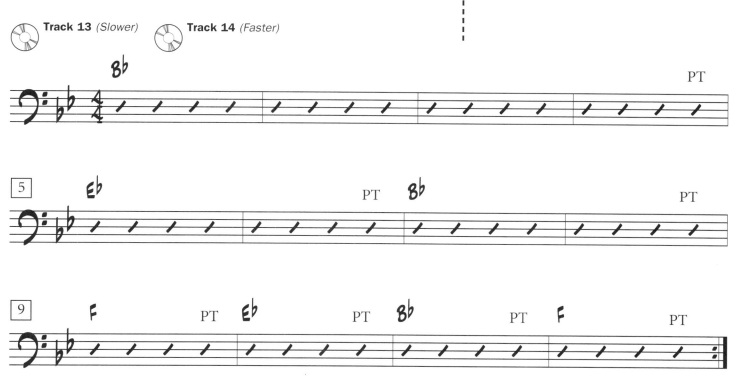

This would also be an excellent time to record yourself again, so that you can listen back to the tracks you've played. See how your notes are lining up with the cymbal beat, and make sure that your time feels steady, with no rushing or hesitations. Listen to your sound also; it should be smooth and rich, with each note sustaining into the next one.

CHAPTER FIVE

LOWER NEIGHBORING TONES
INTRODUCING THE FIFTH AND THE OCTAVE

As you have probably noticed by now, the first four measures of this blues progression are all B♭, which can become a little boring if you play the same chord root over and over. Remember in the first passing tone exercise when I stuck in a couple extra leading tones (the note A) to add variety? Well, you can do the same thing. When you have those first four measures of B♭, slip down and play an A on the fourth beat of any of the first three measures, going right back to the B♭ on the next beat. We could also call this note a *lower neighboring tone*, because we go "next door" down to the note A, and then go right back home to B♭.

TRACKS 15 & 16

Try this: play the progression just as before using either passing tone when the chord changes. Only this time, when you have measures where the chords don't change, slip "next door" (down a fret) on the fourth beat and then go back "home" on the very next beat. The result would look like the example at the top of page 21. Notice that I have marked all the "neighbor" tones with "N." Listen to the examples first, then play along with me before you try dialing out the bass on this one. Note that *all* the passing tones I play in this example are leading tones, approaching the chord root from $1/2$ step below.

21

Track 15 *(Slower)*   **Track 16** *(Faster)*

Another note you can use to spice up long stretches of the same chord is the fifth. The fifth is another chord member, like the root, but we can use it without having to learn all about chord tones and theory. Just look at your bass neck or the diagram below and notice that we can find the fifth of any chord easily. Just learn the pattern: the fifth is found on the adjacent lower string, right across from the root, and on the adjacent higher string, two frets higher. Also notice the pattern on the neck of the low root to the high root, and the low fifth to the high fifth (both are over two strings and up two frets). This distance is called an *octave*.

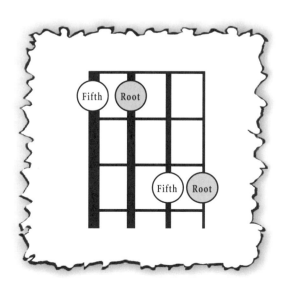

TRACKS 17 & 18

"Okay, I know how to find a fifth, now where do I play it?" That's a fair question, and the answer is "anywhere you want to!" Just remember to play chord roots on the downbeats (the first beat of the measure) especially when the chord changes. Also remember that you have the choice of a higher or lower octave for the B♭ and F chords, so use both. Below is the exact notation of what I played in Tracks 17 & 18. I used nothing but leading tones to get to each chord root from $^1/_2$ step below, and I only used fifths and roots in all other places, just to give you the idea of what you can do by just using these notes and switching octaves now and then.

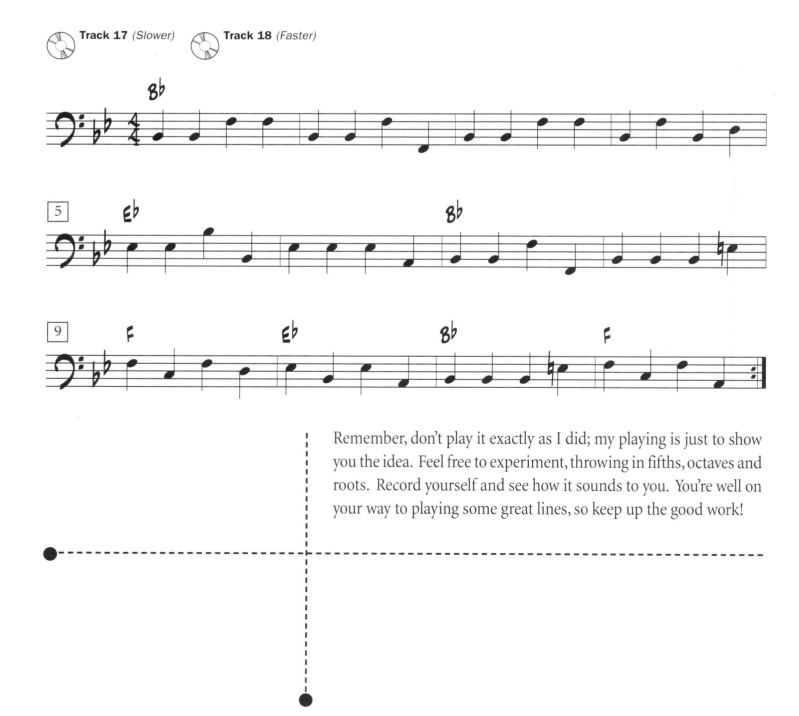

Track 17 *(Slower)*   **Track 18** *(Faster)*

Remember, don't play it exactly as I did; my playing is just to show you the idea. Feel free to experiment, throwing in fifths, octaves and roots. Record yourself and see how it sounds to you. You're well on your way to playing some great lines, so keep up the good work!

All right, it's time to take everything we've learned so far and put it to work for us. We've learned to:

- play chord roots on the first beat of the measure

- approach the next chord root with passing tones from $^1/_2$ step either above or below

- slip "next door" to the note below and back when you have several measures of the same chord

- use fifths and octaves to add variety

CHAPTER SIX

PUTTING IT ALL TOGETHER

TRACKS 19 & 20 (LONGER VERSIONS)

Take these next two tracks and try to put it all together, using all of the devices just listed. Below is the notation of what I played on the first chorus (each time through the progression is called a "chorus"). After that, I'm making it up as I go along, using the concepts we learned, and that's what you should do also. Listen a couple times, then tune me out and go for it. Don't forget to record yourself and check it out.

Track 19 *(Slower)*   **Track 20** *(Faster)*

CHAPTER SEVEN

ADVANCING UPWARD
ADDITIONAL CHORD CHANGES

Now that you have practiced playing through a simple progression in time and used some basic passing tones, let's spice things up a bit by adding a few extra chords to the basic blues progression. Don't panic; the new chords are easy, and they feel very natural.

There are many ways to play a blues chord progression. The one we just learned is very basic, like a rock or blues group might play. This next one is a little more jazzy. Take a look at the chord chart below, and look for the few places where it is different from the one we have been playing.

TRACKS 21 & 22

Don't worry about the "7" added to the chord, it doesn't affect the root. Take a minute to locate the two new chord roots, G and C (measures 8 and 9), on the fingerboard of your bass. Now, take the same techniques we've learned and try playing this progression. Start out easy, with mostly chord roots, then add some passing tones, fifths and octaves.

Track 21 (Slower)   **Track 22** (Faster)

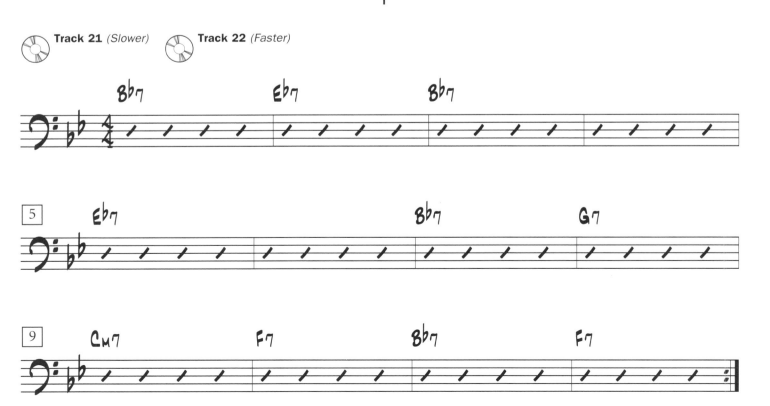

Now, let's take the same progression we've been working on and play it in a different key. This can be difficult on some instruments, but on the bass it's fairly simple. For example, if we were to play a blues in the key of C instead of B♭, we would just move up two frets from B♭ to find our starting note C. Then, all the other patterns we have learned are the same as before. Check out the two diagrams below:

CHAPTER EIGHT
OTHER KEYS

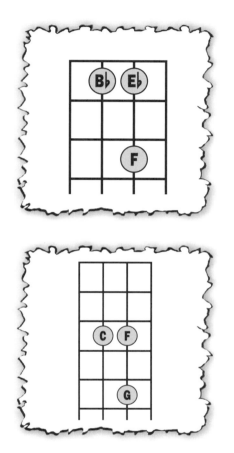

If you have trouble moving to a new key, go back and start the "crawling" process again by just playing chord roots on the downbeats and progressing through the steps from the beginning in the new key. Check out where the notes are on the diagrams, and locate them on your instrument. Try this blues progression in the key of C.

TRACK 23 You can use this step-by-step process to learn how to play walking bass lines on any new chord progressions.

Track 23

TRACK 24

This track is another blues, but this time in the key of F. Just think of F as your starting point, find all of the chord roots on the neck, and give it a go. Notice the added chords (circled) in the last two measures. This is called a "*turnaround*," and it's a nifty little way to lead back to the top of the chorus. The chords come a bit faster, every two beats, so start out by playing just roots on the turnaround, then add passing tones. You can approach each chord root from either above or below, so try each, then mix it up and use both. Listen to my bass line in the turnaround to see how I do it, then go ahead and try it yourself. This turnaround idea isn't limited to the blues; in fact, most songs that have a repeating form have some sort of turnaround to get back to the top smoothly, so practice this. It is something you will use over and over again.

Track 24

Another more advanced technique you can try is adding an extra passing tone. For example, instead of just one note moving to the next chord root from a $^{1}/_{2}$ step away (either above or below), try playing *two* half steps to get there. Play the note two half steps away on beat three, the note one half step away on beat four, and the chord root itself on beat one. Look at the examples below. In both examples, I'm playing just chord roots except for the two half step approach tones, just to show the idea clearly. Track 25 uses approach tones from below the target chord root, and Track 26 uses approach tones from above it. Listen to these tracks on the CD, play along with me when you think you understand the concept, then dial me out and try it on your own.

Notice in the turnaround there is only one approach tone, not two. This is because in the turnaround, you only have *one* beat between each new chord root, so there is only room for *one* approach note.

CHAPTER NINE

EXTRA PASSING TONES

TRACK 25

Track 25

TRACK 26

Track 26

In Chapter 10, I play acoustic bass on all the examples, so you can hear how a walking bass line sounds on this instrument. Many of the walking bass lines you hear on recordings are played on acoustic bass, and this is the sound I try to imitate when I play a walking line on the electric bass

CHAPTER
TEN

**MASTERING
THE WALKING
BASS LINE**

This closing chapter contains the key to the last five tracks on the CD. The first three are blues cuts in three different keys, Bb, C and F. The tracks are longer than before, so you can really practice your ability to concentrate and keep the energy going, which is very important in a real playing situation. These last tracks are also a bit faster than before, just to keep you on your toes.

Track 30 is a common type of progression where the chords resolve down a fifth. It is really only an eight-measure exercise in the key of C with each chord lasting two measures. The eight-measure pattern then repeats several times so you can really concentrate on locking-in with the drummer and trying all the various types of passing tones we've discussed.

Track 31 is a 32-measure tune based on the chord changes to "No Greater Love." This is a longer form than the blues, which is only 12 measures, but three of the phrases are pretty much the same, and one is different. We call this type of form an AABA form, and those letters show which parts are the same and which parts are different. This tune is also in Bb, which should be very familiar to you by now.

Have fun with these last five tracks. Remember to concentrate and keep the time steady and locked in with the cymbal beat. Listen to my bass part a few times, then dial me out. Try recording yourself with these tracks just as though you were in a recording studio. Listen back to your playing; this process will teach you exactly what you need to practice. Enjoy yourself, and GOOD LUCK!

TRACK 27

Track 27

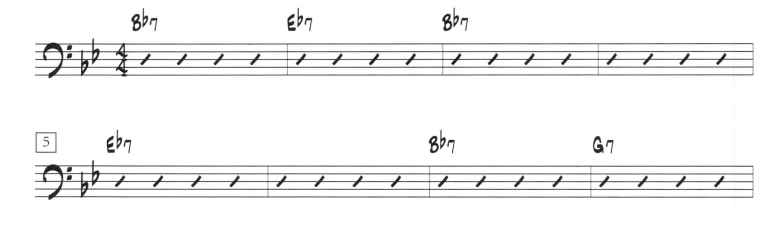

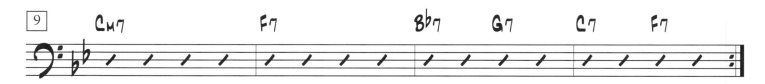

TRACK 28

Track 28

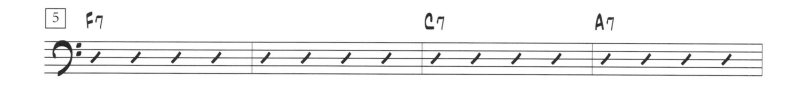

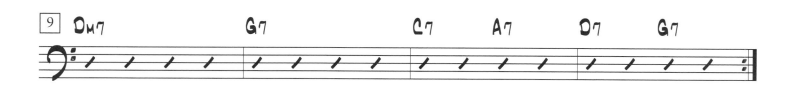

TRACK 29

Track 29

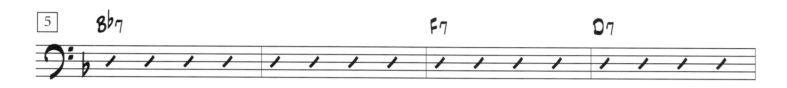

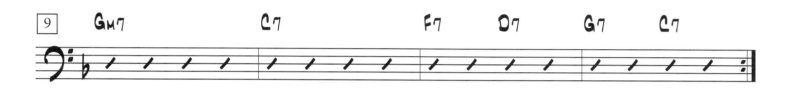

TRACK 30

Track 30

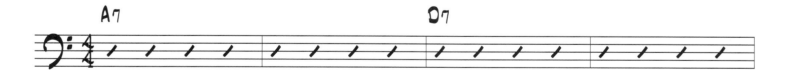

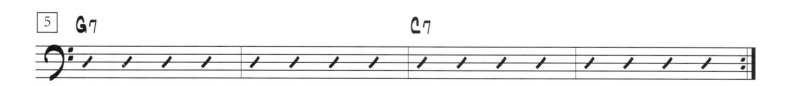

TRACK 31 • IN THE STYLE OF "NO GREATER LOVE"   Track 31